Women

of the

Bible

Sherry Bliss Haase

ISBN 979-8-88685-367-4 (paperback)
ISBN 979-8-88685-368-1 (digital)

Christian Faith Publishing
832 Park Avenue
Meadville, PA 16335
www.christianfaithpublishing.com

Author's photo by Debbie Stockwell Studio

Printed in the United States of America

To my Lord and Savior, Jesus Christ,
who led me on this journey.
And to my wonderful family and friends
who supported me through it.

Contents

Foreword...vii

Women We Can Relate To 1

    Eve 3

    Leah 7

    Ten Virgins—Five Foolish and Five Wise 11

Influential Women of the Bible 15

    Deborah and Jael...................................17

    Esther 21

    Lydia 25

Biblical Wives...29

    Abigail..31

    Sapphira 35

    Proverbs 31 Wife 39

Female Relationships 43

    Peninnah 45

    Hannah 49

    Ruth 53

    Naomi 57

Women in Jesus's Inner Circle 61

   Mary, Mother of Jesus..................................63

   Martha 67

   Mary, Sister of Lazarus and Martha 71

Stories of Redemption 75

   Rahab...77

   Gomer..81

   Zelophehad's Daughters
   (Mahlah, Noah, Hoglah, Milcah, and Tirzah)......85

Foreword

Hello, sisters,

I am truly honored you chose to read this book as part of your spiritual journey. A few years ago, the Lord prompted me to write a devotional which studied women in the Bible. Although these women lived thousands of years ago, we have much to learn from their stories. Some women have characteristics we want to emulate, others not so much. This is not a book written by a master theologian or a woman who has it all together. It is a devotional written by a broken believer, sharing her perspective of stories in the Bible in an authentic and relatable manner.

As a working mom juggling multiple obligations, I understand the difficulty of keeping all the balls in the air. I also have learned the value of spending time in the Word daily. I have never been a morning person, but I've found getting up a little earlier to enjoy a cup of coffee and devotional before the rest of my house awakes has become my treasured time.

While doing this study, you will need a Bible (or Bible app) and a journal. Each lesson should take about fifteen to thirty minutes (depending on how much you like to journal) and will involve a scripture reading, my commentary, and questions to help apply the lessons to our lives. The devotional can be done individually or as a group. I hope it will encourage you to delve into scripture and grow in your walk with Christ, knowing you are not alone. May God bless you!

For the group leader,

When using this devotional for a group Bible study, my suggestion would be to focus on one of the six themes each week, choosing one to two questions from each lesson to prompt discussion.

Women We Can Relate To

From the beginning of time, we see women experiencing emotions we still struggle with today—temptation, hurt, feeling inadequate, and making poor choices we regret later. In this section, we will watch Eve fall into Satan's temptation, empathize with Leah, whose husband was in love with her sister, and consider the consequences of the ill-prepared women in the parable of the ten virgins.

Eve

Genesis 3:1–7

Eve, the first woman, the first wife, the first mother. Most of us are familiar with this story. For me, it's not only because I've heard it many times, but I've also lived it more often than I would like to admit, falling into temptation and making bad decisions that go against God's instructions.

At first glance, Eve's motivation behind her sin does not necessarily seem bad, to be wise, and to be more like God; however, she placed her desire to be like God above her desire to follow God. Attempting to elevate her status by disobeying His commands, she fell into sin. If we are presented with a situation where the end results seem positive, but the means to achieve them go against what the Bible says, a warning flag should go up in our minds. We need to consult God in our decision-making process through prayer, scripture, and seeking wise counsel when appropriate.

God's commands are put in place to protect us and bring us closer to Him. Sometimes this is easy to see. For example, "Do not commit adultery." We know (either firsthand or by witnessing others go through it) the pain that infidelity causes. It makes sense to avoid it. However, other times, we don't see the reasoning behind God's teachings, which can make them feel restrictive. Here is when it becomes tempting to disregard them. We must trust God's infinite knowledge and believe His instructions are for our good even when we don't understand why.

Eve's actions also showed a lack of contentment. God gave her and Adam a garden full of delicious fruit trees. Why did she need to eat from the off-limits one? When we focus on what we don't have instead of what God has provided us, discontentment can set in and alter our decisions. The greatest antidote for discontentment is gratitude. When we are giving thanks to God, our focus shifts away from what feel we are lacking and onto our abundant blessings.

Let's not forget Satan's role in this.

> Stay alert! Watch out for your great enemy, the devil. He prowls around like a roaring lion, looking for someone to devour.
>
> (1 Peter 5:8 NLT)

The tactics he used with Eve continue to work for him today. Satan can convince us to give in to our temptations by preying on our discontentment and trying to convince us that God is withholding good things from us. We need to be on guard against his deception and be aware of our areas of weakness that he can potentially use to tempt us into sin and separate us from God.

1. Do you identify with Eve? How so?
2. Are there commands in the Bible that you have a hard time following because you don't understand the reason for them?
3. Can you identify areas of weakness in your life that could make it easy to fall into temptation?
4. What is one thing you can do to help combat discontentment and resist temptation?

____

____

____

____

____

____

____

____

Leah

Genesis 29:14b–35

While reading this story, what may first stand out is Laban cheating Jacob and denying him and Rachel their marriage after Jacob fulfilled his commitment of working for Laban, *sans* pay, for seven years. There is another victim here, Leah. Can you imagine what it must have felt like to know your husband is really in love with your sister? To know that on your wedding day, your husband was filled with shock and disappointment, instead of joy. Talk about devastation (not to mention family dysfunction).

Have you ever felt like second best? Or maybe even third or fourth or fifth best? Perhaps it was growing up in a family where one of your siblings was clearly the favorite. Or maybe you had a boyfriend who just wasn't ready to settle down (he swore it had nothing to do with you), then you find out a few months after your breakup that he's engaged. Or maybe the excitement of your new job waned when you learned that their first choice had turned down the offer.

Let's face it, it does not feel good to come in behind someone else, but I have good news. There is one area where you will come in number one every…single…time. When God created (fill in your name here), you were his first pick, hands down. He created you, with your unique gifts and talents, exactly as He intended you to be.

Take a moment to think about your gifts and talents. This may be uncomfortable for us. It may feel braggadocious to claim we are *gifted* in a certain way; however, God does give each of us unique gifts and talents that He wants us to use for His glory. I will get personal for a moment. God has gifted me with a gregarious personality. I know this has benefitted me in my career and even more importantly in relationships. I am blessed with many great friends. I also believe that I have a responsibility in using this gift by reaching out to others, for example, being friendly to someone who looks uncomfortable in a new situation, volunteering as a greeter at church, or inviting someone to an event or into my home. Sometimes it may be as simple as bringing joy to someone's day with a sincere compliment. I frequently tell complete strangers how much I like their hair or their dress, often to my children's chagrin. ("Mom, do you have to talk to everyone?")

On another note, if you are currently in a position where someone is constantly making you feel like you don't measure up, I would recommend you pray about the situation and evaluate where you need to take action. Do you work for a boss who is constantly belittling you? If so, you may want to consider exploring other employment options. Are you in a friendship or dating relationship with someone who acts like you are not worthy of them? God calls us to love everyone; however, there may be times where we need to set boundaries or end a toxic relationship. If the person who is making you feel like you are not good enough is your spouse, I know this is an extremely painful place to be. I would suggest addressing this issue by talking to your spouse to let them know how you feel or seeking marital counseling to try to improve your relationship. Always remember your heavenly Father created you, loves you, and welcomes you into His royal family. You are worthy!

1. Have you ever felt like second best? Do you still have pain or feelings of inadequacy because of it? If so, what steps do you need to take to allow healing in this area?
2. Take a moment to list out some of your God-given gifts.
3. How are you using those gifts today?
4. Is God prompting you to use your abilities in a new way?

____

____

____

____

____

____

Ten Virgins— Five Foolish and Five Wise

Matthew 25:1–13

Jesus tells this story to illustrate the importance of being spiritually prepared when the time comes for Him to take His people to heaven. In this example, He is the bridegroom, and the marriage feast represents heaven. The five foolish bridesmaids, who were not prepared, were not allowed into the feast, just as those who do not accept Jesus as their Savior are not welcomed into heaven.

This parable about being spiritually prepared makes me think of my salvation story. I grew up in the Catholic church and always believed in God; however, I wouldn't say I had a close, personal relationship with Him. In my early twenties, I was going to mass regularly, but my heart was not in it. I viewed it as a task to check off each week. To be honest, spiritual growth was not a priority at that time. I was going through a bit of a wild period in my life. I was partying every weekend, typically drinking way too much alcohol. God protected me from many stupid decisions that put me in vulnerable situations, like accepting drinks and rides home with guys I barely knew.

A friend invited me to a new church. I enjoyed the services but remember thinking that I wasn't ready to become a Christian just yet. I wasn't ready to be "that good." I wanted to have fun for a little longer and then settle down. That same friend explained to me that salvation wasn't something you had to clean yourself up for. God meets us wherever we are. Salvation is about believing that Jesus is the Son of God, and He came to earth to die on a cross so that our sins would be forgiven. Whoever believes in Him will receive the gift of eternal life. All we have to do is accept this precious gift. I love how Paul describes it:

> We are made right with God by placing our faith in Jesus Christ. And this is true for everyone who believes, no matter who we are. For everyone has sinned; we all fall short of God's glorious standard. Yet God, in his grace, freely makes us right in his sight. He did this through Christ Jesus when he freed us from the penalty for our sins.
>
> (Romans 3:22–24 NLT)

I knew that I believed this, so that night, I said a prayer, accepting Jesus as my Lord and Savior. After that day, God gradually made changes in me. I no longer had the desire to get drunk every weekend. Going to church became something I looked forward to, rather than something I was supposed to do.

As I started to mature spiritually, grow closer to God, and make wiser decisions, I realized how much better life was with Jesus by my side. I'm glad Jesus didn't come to take His people to heaven during that rebellious time of my life when I felt like I needed to have a little more fun before committing to Him. I don't know if I would have been invited. Life is precious. We truly don't know when our last day will be. We must always be prepared to meet with God. My goal at the end of my life here on earth, whether that is next week or in fifty years, is to have Jesus welcome me into heaven, saying, "Well done, good and faithful servant." It's not about being perfect. It's about being in a relationship with our Savior and realizing our life is better when we are following Him.

1. Think about when you first accepted the gift of salvation. Did you notice God nudging you to make changes in your life to bring you closer to him? If you have not accepted this gift yet, I encourage you to think about what reservations you have and pray honestly to God. Trust me, He can take it.
2. Are there changes in your life that are needed right now to bring you closer to God?
3. What feelings arise when you think about what happens after your life here on earth is finished?
4. Is there someone in your life who has not accepted the gift of salvation with whom you can be sharing your faith?

SHERRY BLISS HAASE

Influential Women of the Bible

Prepare to be inspired as we read the stories of how God used the unique gifts of battle warriors Deborah and Jael, Queen Esther, and hostess Lydia to advance His kingdom. These women were in unique positions to glorify God and bring others to Him. I hope that this section will help you reflect on your God-given talents and how to use them to serve Him and others.

Deborah and Jael

Judges 4:1–24

If you're looking for a little biblical girl power, Judges 4 is a good place to go. Here, we see examples of women in positions of leadership and power, not common to that period of history. Let's start with Deborah, our boss girl of the Bible. First, we see that Deborah is a respected judge. Say what? I didn't think that was even allowed back then. Then we find out she was also a prophet. I believe that for her to be respected in these roles during this era shows that she was in a God-ordained position. When she shares with Barak the message the Lord gave to her about going into battle against King Jabin and his commander, Sisera, there was no doubt the instructions came from the Lord. He did, however, ask Deborah to accompany him. Add military leader to Deborah's resume. Barak continued to follow her counsel as they went into battle. Barak, Deborah, and their army were victorious over Sisera's warriors, but Sisera himself escaped.

Here was where Jael came in. Sisera attempted to take refuge in her tent because her husband was friendly with King Jabin. God gave Jael the opportunity to defeat the enemy, and she took it. I believe the fact that she was a woman aided in the success of the mission. Sisera did not even consider her a threat. She went on to make him feel more comfortable covering him with a blanket and giving him milk. After all, we women are known to be nurturing and hospitable. If one of Barak's male soldiers was in that tent, you can bet that Sisera would not have even gone in, let alone asked to be tucked in for a little nap. Jael recognized the unique position she was in and bravely fulfilled Deborah's prophesy, "For the Lord's victory over Sisera will be at the hands of a woman" (Judges 4:9).

In the next chapter of Judges, Deborah and Barak sang a song of praise. Deborah gave full recognition of their success to God. Her goal was not to promote herself or even show what women are capable of. She saw herself as God's messenger, willing to be used in whatever capacity He needed her and gave all the glory to Him.

I've heard many people say the Bible is oppressive to women. I believe that the oppression comes more from the culture of the time, not from God. We see several examples in the Bible where God is revolutionary, using women in ways that completely go against the social norms of that day and age. God created every person, male and female, in His likeness. God has given each of us gifts to be used for His glory. If God prompts you to use a unique gift, do not let old stereotypes deter you. If God wants to use you in this manner, trust that He will bring you through it.

It is a different world today, thankfully, where women's gifts are recognized, and they are encouraged to be leaders. It is important to show young women these biblical examples where God uses women in unique ways to glorify Him and advance His kingdom.

1. What gifts do you believe God has given you to glorify His kingdom?
2. Have you ever been discouraged from using one of your gifts because of your age, gender, or ethnicity?
3. Do you have the gift of leadership? If so, what are some ways that you can use it?
4. Is there a girl in your life who would be encouraged by the brave actions of Deborah and Jael? If so, make a point to share this story with them.

____

____

____

____

____

____

____

Esther

Esther 2:1–18, 4:6–17

At first, when we hear about Esther spending a year residing at the king's palace with seven maids, receiving daily beauty treatments, it can sound a little dreamy. However, I don't think it was exactly a spa-like experience. These beauty treatments were all done to groom these young women to *please* the king. The girls in the harem waited until the king was ready to use them for his sexual pleasure. I can imagine what went through these young minds, wondering what would be expected of them when their time came.

Esther is a beautiful example of courage and discernment. She uses her influence as the chosen queen to save her people. She is wise about how she approaches the difficult and potentially dangerous tasks in front of her. When we are faced with a difficult situation that we need to address, for example, an uncomfortable conversation or standing up for something we know is right but will alienate some people, acting in a discerning manner can be a challenge. I've noticed that people usually fall into two camps: those who like to tackle the situation head-on, "rip off the band-aid" to get the whole thing over with, and those who want to bury their head in the sand and hope that the ugly situation will go away.

Although I'm guilty of using both of these tactics, I tend to fall into the first camp. I hate having things hang over my head. I like to have issues done and settled. This method can lead to acting impulsively, on high emotions, jumping into a situation or conversation ill-prepared, and likely at a time where it may not be well received. ("Wow, Sherry! I see how that would upset you. I'm very sorry for how it caused you to feel and am *so* glad you brought it up just as I walked through the door after a stressful day at work," said my husband. NEVER.)

God is working on my patience. Avoidance, however, has its own set of consequences, and bad situations don't always resolve themselves. Fear and anxiety can prevent us from doing what needs to be done. There is a middle ground between acting rashly and procrastinating. Esther got it right. Her first reaction was fear, completely understandable considering approaching the king uninvited could lead to death. (I probably would not have lasted long as queen in his palace.) However, she realized what was at stake and the unique position she was in to save her people. She prayed. She fasted. She reached out for additional support, sending a message to Mordecai asking her people to pray and fast as well. Bravely, willing to risk her life, she approached the king humbly and waited for the right time to make her request.

I encourage you to read the entire book of Esther in the Bible, full of drama and plot twists. Spoiler alert: Things end well for Esther and her people. Lord, please give me patience, courage, wisdom, and discernment like Esther.

1. How do you tend to react when faced with a difficult or uncomfortable situation?
2. Has there been a time in your life when acting impulsively inflamed an already-tense relationship?
3. Is there an issue in your life right now that you have avoided addressing? What can you do to face the problem appropriately? I would encourage you to pray for wisdom. If you are unsure how to best approach the issue, seek counsel and support from a trusted friend or mentor.

Bonus reading: The book of Esther

____

____

____

____

____

____

Lydia

Acts 16:12–15, 40
Matthew 25:34–40

In Lydia, we see a biblical example of a successful businesswoman. Let's be honest, this is a bit of a rare find. Lydia's story shows how God uses women in various roles and positions to grow His kingdom. Because Paul mentions she was "a merchant of expensive purple cloth" and had a "household" (which likely included servants), we can assume she was a woman of means. She was a Jewish woman who worshipped God; and when she heard Paul speak, God opened her heart to believe Jesus Christ was the promised Messiah. She must have been prompted to share this good news since not only did Lydia declare her faith through baptism, her household did as well. I picture her filled with the Holy Spirit, on fire for the Lord, bursting to share the Gospel with everyone around her.

Immediately after the baptism, Lydia was anxious to serve God and these missionaries with what she had by insisting they stay in her home. She demonstrates how hospitality is a form of worship. Opening our home to others, whether it is by inviting a friend for coffee, hosting a Bible study, or giving someone in need a place to stay, we are not only showing Christ's love to others but also serving Jesus himself. We learn this in Matthew 25 when He tells us that by feeding, clothing, and sheltering the least of His brothers and sisters, we are providing food, clothing, and shelter to Him.

There was a time when I was a young adult, in between living situations, my friend, Danielle, and her husband, Ken, offered to let me (and my cat) stay in their guest room for a couple of months, while I figured out where I was going to move next. Twenty years later, I still remember how welcome they made me feel and appreciate their kind hospitality during a stressful season of my life.

Although there are not many verses dedicated specifically to Lydia, we know that Paul stayed at her home multiple times, including when he and Silas were released from prison. During this time, it says they met with other believers and encouraged them. Lydia's home was a place where believers gathered in the earliest days of the church. Though her name is not specifically mentioned, I believe Lydia is one of the people Paul so fondly writes to in the first chapter of Philippians. Because of her willing heart, God used Lydia to spread the message of Jesus Christ and grow His church.

1. Is hospitality one of your spiritual gifts? If so, what are some ways you may be able to use it to serve Jesus and others?
2. We sense Lydia being on fire for the Lord after hearing Paul's message by the way she witnessed to her household and jumped into serving. Do you

remember when you were first saved? Did you have this same enthusiasm as Lydia, excited to share the Gospel and eager to serve God?

3. Sometimes in our Christian walk, we can get stuck in a rut, and our worship and ministry become routine. If you are feeling this way, write down some ways you can reignite your relationship with the Lord. Consider joining a small group, trying a new ministry, or sharing the Gospel with someone God has brought into your life.

Bonus reading: Philippians 1:1–10

Biblical Wives

The Bible has many examples of married couples. In the stories of Abigail and Sapphira, we witness two wives with very different responses to their husbands' sins. Proverbs 31 gives us a picture of an ideal wife described by King Lemuel's mother as she advises him in selecting his future bride.

Abigail

1 Samuel 25:1–42

Abigail, a wise and brave peacemaker, is in a difficult place, being married to Nabal who is not a man of good character. Nabal's refusal to adhere to David's request for provisions completely went against the social customs of this time. Hospitality toward travelers was expected, especially under circumstances like this, where David and his men had protected Nabal's assets, contributing to his wealth. His refusal demonstrates greed and a lack of moral compass. We are told in verse 3 that Abigail, unlike her husband, possessed wisdom and character. The way the servant speaks to Abigail, in verses 14–17, shows us that others were aware of this.

The servant recognized Abigail as perhaps the only person who was in a position to prevent the attack. When Abigail heard about how her husband responded to David's messengers, she recognized the potential consequences and acted quickly. Abigail must have had a catering staff at her disposal to pull off the preparation of the food needed for David and his army. She bravely and humbly went to meet with David herself to diffuse the contentious situation.

Abigail understood that it was not just her husband's life in danger, but the lives of his entire staff. Knowing her husband, she decided not to let him know her plan, a decision that saved hundreds of lives.

We can assume by the events that happened next that Abigail prayed and sought God's wisdom in this. David recognized that Abigail was sent by God to prevent the bloodshed which was about to occur. When Nabal died of a heart attack after hearing about his wife's actions, David took Abigail to be his wife. The marriage was a blessing to Abigail since living as a widow during that time was extremely difficult. The Lord provided for His daughter.

This lesson was hard for me to write because unfortunately, I expect that some of you reading this book may be in a similar situation, living with a difficult husband. My heart goes out to you. I pray that the Lord will give you wisdom in your circumstances. I hope that you have someone in your life you can go to, a pastor, a trusted friend, or a professional counselor. If not, I urge you to find one.

Even if we are not married to someone like Nabal, our husbands, like us, are human. There are times when high emotions cause them to act irrationally or inappropriately. In these situations, we may be a calming influence and help them see things more reasonably. (My husband and I are both very emotional people. I hope that at any given moment, at least one of us will be thinking rationally. This doesn't always happen.) There may even be times where, like Abigail, we need to intervene on their behalf. Tread lightly in this area. Examine your reasons why you feel like you need to intervene. Is it because your husband is doing something illegal or unbiblical? Or is it simply because you disagree with him? I am not suggesting going behind your husband's back. If it falls into the illegal or unbiblical territory, and you have tried talking to your husband to no avail, I urge you to stay in prayer and seek wise counsel about potential action you should take.

Situations vary greatly. I am not in a position to give blanket advice here. What we can all glean from Abigail's story is the power of a woman seeking peace. The character she showed, using her influence wisely, saved many lives. We will have opportunities throughout our lives where we are in a position to be a peacemaker, whether it be among family and friends or in our place of work, even within the church. If you find yourself in the middle of a tense situation where you may have influence, pray for how you might be able to sow seeds of peace.

1. Do you think Abigail was justified in going behind her husband's back? Why?
2. Has there ever been a time when you have felt the need to intervene on your husband's behalf? How did you handle the situation?
3. What can you do to be a positive influence on your husband and others around you?
4. Are you in a situation right now where God could use you as a peacemaker? How can you help spread peace?

34

Sapphira

Acts 5:1–11
Matthew 6:2–4

It is interesting that in the first two verses, Luke, the author of Acts, points out not once but twice that Sapphira was as much a part of this act of deceit as her husband. I cannot help but wonder why Ananias and Sapphira felt the need to lie about the amount of money they gave after selling their property. It was their property to do with as they pleased. I assume whatever amount they claimed to have received for the land would be a very generous gift. So again, why lie? Was it to make themselves look better in the eyes of the apostles? They could not possibly think that they were fooling God, could they? It seems like their giving was out of pride and for the sake of appearance.

It is human nature to want recognition. I certainly enjoy a pat on the back for doing something good. Peter asks, "Ananias, why has Satan filled your heart?" Satan knows our human weaknesses and will prey on them when given the chance. We need to be careful not to let him get a foothold in areas where we struggle. When we give to others, whether it be our time or monetary resources, it can be tempting to make sure our deed does not go unnoticed. God, however, sees it differently. He wants our gifts made solely out of a desire to please Him. Jesus addressed this pretty clearly in Matthew 6. God sees everything we do. He knows our thoughts and our hearts. When we give to honor Him and not out of a desire to look good, He is pleased. Second Corinthians 9:7 states that "God loves a cheerful giver."

Although we are not privy to the conversations and conspiracy that went on between Ananias and Sapphira, we do know that she was on board with the deception and lied when Peter asked her about the price of the land. The Bible speaks about showing your husband respect, but this does not include supporting them on something you know is sinful. If you are in a situation where your husband is asking you to be a part of something you believe is wrong, I would advise you to let him know your feelings about the situation and seek additional counsel if necessary. Perhaps getting your pastor or another trusted Christian involved will help him, as well as you, see the situation more clearly. I realize that some of you may have a husband who is not a believer, which makes things even more difficult. As wives, we are called to pray for our husbands and be a positive influence on them.

1. Have you ever given a gift or done a good deed completely anonymously? How did it make you feel?
2. What are things you struggle with wanting recognition?
3. Is it tempting to lie to make yourself look better?

Proverbs 31 Wife

Proverbs 31:10–31

In today's devotion, we are not reading about an actual woman but rather a picture of an ideal wife through the advice given to King Lemuel by his mother. At first glance, this scripture can be overwhelming. As a newlywed, I remember wanting to discreetly remove this page from my husband's Bible so he would not think this standard was even remotely realistic. But as I dig deeper and consider the context behind these words, a few things stand out.

The first is the personal qualities that are esteemed when describing this woman. The king's wise mama tries conveying to her son the importance of choosing a wife based on character over physical beauty. This ideal wife is praised for her virtue, as well as her capabilities. Not once is her physical appearance mentioned. In today's society, there is so much emphasis placed on a person's looks. These verses remind us of the fleetingness of our outer shell and the qualities we should be looking for instead when considering our future spouse.

The second lesson I gleaned from this scripture is that it demonstrates the variety of talents and potential roles a woman might hold. The example given describes a devoted wife and mother, a thoughtful employer, and a savvy businesswoman. She is industrious, organized, and hardworking. She is a planner, someone who looks ahead, and is well prepared. She is respected by her family and her community and, most importantly, fears the LORD.

Many people mistakenly believe that the Bible's ideal woman is meek and solely domestic. Here, we see a woman using her talents in a variety of ways. As women, we have many paths available to us. Our priorities and focus may shift as we go through life. When I was in my twenties, my career was a heavy focus. At thirty-one, when my son was born, I felt called to step away from my job and stay at home full-time. It was a good decision for me and my family. As my children got older, resuming my career, initially through part-time work, then eventually full-time, felt right. Other women feel called to work outside the home while raising children. God's plan for some women may not include a husband or children. God gives each of us unique talents and provides opportunities to use them in different seasons of our lives to glorify Him and serve others through our family, careers, and ministry.

When I read these verses now, instead of seeing this as an impossible standard to measure up to, I see it as an encouragement to use the talents I have been given and work excellently in whatever roles I am currently assigned. It reminds me that cultivating my character and inner beauty is far more important than my outward appearance, and honoring God should always come first.

Charm is deceptive, and beauty does
not last; but a woman who fears the Lord
will be greatly praised.

(Proverbs 31:30 NLT)

1. How do you feel after reading these verses?
   Inspired? Overwhelmed?
2. What can we do in our beauty-obsessed culture to
   value character over appearance?
3. How are you able to glorify God and serve others
   in your current role?
4. If you have children who are not yet married, what
   are some qualities you hope for in their future
   spouse? Do you discuss them with your child? Do
   you pray for their future spouse?

____

____

____

____

____

____

____

Female Relationships

In this section, we will study two very different female relationships. First, we read about Hannah and the cruel treatment she receives from Peninnah, another wife of her husband, Elkanah. In sharp contrast, Ruth's love and loyalty toward her mother-in-law, Naomi, depicts a beautiful example of the value female relationships can bring to our lives.

Peninnah

1 Samuel 1

Although Hannah's story is the primary focus of this scripture (don't worry, we will be talking about this godly woman next), I think there is a lesson as we read about Peninnah. The first thing that comes to my mind when I think of Peninnah is *mean girl!* (Truthfully, there is another word that pops into my mind first, but it is inappropriate to write inside a Bible study.)

Having experienced the struggle of infertility, including two miscarriages, before being blessed with my two beautiful, healthy children, I can relate to the heartbreak that Hannah experienced. Thankfully, I did not have a Peninnah in my life to rub salt into my wounds. It was sometimes painful enough having people who loved me, with the best intentions, try to give me *words of comfort.* (Side note: If you have a loved one who has just experienced a miscarriage, telling them, "It's for the best," is probably not what they want to hear at that moment.)

Let's ponder what may have caused Peninnah to act cruelly toward Hannah. I believe much of it stems from her jealousy and insecurity. From what we read in the scripture, Hannah would appear to be the favorite of their husband, Elkanah. Imagine how irritated Peninnah felt when she saw Hannah getting the double portion of meat and other ways Elkanah may have shown her more affection. She took out her feelings on Hannah, taunting her with the one thing she had over Hannah, which was also the one thing Hannah desired the most.

Sisters, we have the opportunity to lift each other up or tear each other down. Let's be careful not to let our feelings of jealousy and insecurity cause us to attack or judge other women. Marriage is hard. Motherhood is hard. Life is hard. It is so much better to journey with authentic girlfriends by our sides that will lift us, laugh with us, and cry with us, especially in our darkest times.

Surround yourself with these women and be that woman to others. If you do have a *Peninnah* in your life, you may not be able to control their words and actions, but you can control how they affect you. The adage, "Hurting people, hurt people," is true. Their words and actions likely have more to do with their issues than with you. Jesus tells us to "love our enemies" (one of his most difficult commandments, for sure). However, it is okay to set healthy boundaries with toxic people. Love them and pray for them, but be cautious about letting their words and actions affect your emotional well-being.

1. Have you ever had a Peninnah in your life? How did you handle it?
2. How can we love our enemies while still establishing boundaries to protect our emotional well-being?

3. Who are the authentic female friendships in your life for whom you are thankful?
4. Write down some things you can do this week to foster those relationships.

If you feel like you are missing authentic female relationships in your life right now, pray for God to bring a special friend into your life. Write down one thing you can do this week to reach out in this area. For example, inquire about women's small groups at your church, reconnect with a dear friend you have lost touch with, or invite someone to coffee.

____

____

____

____

____

____

____

Hannah

There is so much to glean from Hannah's story. Because of my experience, I can appreciate the pain her barrenness caused her. From a young age, my desire to be a mother was strong. When the time seemed right for my husband and me to start our family, I was shocked when it did not happen as quickly as I thought it would. Each month brought new hope, then bitter disappointment. Watching my friends experience the joy of motherhood was bittersweet. I was sincerely happy for them, but jealous too. The years of waiting for our dreams of parenthood to be fulfilled were highly emotional.

Hannah got to the point where she was so distraught she could not even eat. In her anguish, she went to the Lord, poured out her soul, and made a promise that if God were to bless her with a son, she would give him back to the Lord for his entire lifetime. God grants her prayer. She keeps her promise. This part of the story breaks my heart. How hard it must have been, after finally receiving the beautiful baby boy she had been longing for all those years, to leave him to serve the Lord.

I am dreading letting go of my children at age eighteen. I cannot imagine leaving a toddler. Her prayer of praise as she dedicates Samuel's life to God and prepares to leave him shows the state of her mind and heart. What an act of faith, obedience, trust, and honoring a promise! Hannah recognized that all of our gifts, even our children, are on loan from God. This concept can be hard to digest and put into practice, especially when we are talking about our babies.

Samuel grew up as the Lord's helper, an apprentice priest under Eli. He went on to be Israel's greatest judge. Hannah visited him each year and brought a new little tunic she had made for him. (I get misty-eyed reading about this sweet act.) As painful as it was for her to give him up, how proud she must have felt watching him mature and serve the Lord. God rewarded Hannah for keeping her promise. The woman who spent all of those years longing for a child was blessed with three more sons and two daughters at an age people would have believed was too late to conceive.

God's timing often does not align with ours, but we need to trust His plan is better. I look at my son and my daughter and feel so blessed. The difficult years of infertility make me appreciate these precious children, meant to be ours, on loan from God, in His perfect timing.

1. Have you had a dream that you gave up on only to have God fulfill it in His perfect timing? How did that process affect your faith, both during the

disappointing period and when your hopes were eventually fulfilled?

2. Have you ever made a promise you wished you could take back?

3. Do you struggle with the concept that our blessings are on loan to us but ultimately belong to God?

4. What things in your life are the hardest to let go of?

____

____

____

____

____

____

____

____

52

Ruth

Ruth 1:3–2:12

This story gives us a beautiful example of a human relationship, exemplifying love, devotion, and caring for one another. Considering it is between a mother-in-law and daughter-in-law, which can often be a complicated dynamic, makes it even more remarkable. Naomi's insistence that Ruth and Orpah return to their homeland for a better opportunity to remarry and have children shows her selflessness. I'm sure she would much prefer to have her daughters-in-law accompany her on her journey back to Judah, but she was looking out for their best interest. I certainly don't fault Orpah for adhering to Naomi's practical advice (I hate to admit it, but I would likely have done the same thing.) But I completely admire Ruth's fierce loyalty in refusing to leave Naomi. It's not surprising that Ruth's words of dedication in chapter 1, verses 16 to 17 are often included in wedding ceremonies.

Once they arrived in Bethlehem, Ruth continued to care for Naomi, taking the initiative to go and gather left-over grain for the two of them to eat. We see God rewarding Ruth and providing for her and Naomi as she ends up in the field of Boaz, a relative of Naomi's late husband. Boaz shows his appreciation for Ruth's care of Naomi, telling her to stay and glean in his field where she would be protected.

In this day and age in our country, people don't always take care of their families the same way they did in the past and don't necessarily view their in-laws in the same way they view their own family. It's not as common for multiple generations to live under the same roof. We may live in a whole different city or state from our extended family members, but even so, we have the responsibility to take care of our families and others in need. Let Ruth be an example of how we treat our relatives and people in vulnerable positions.

1. Reflect on the decision Ruth and Orpah each faced when Naomi insists they return to their homeland. What would you have done?
2. Has there been a time in your life when you made a difficult decision and God later rewarded you?
3. In this story, we see Ruth helping Naomi, then Boaz helping Ruth. Think of a time when someone helped you when you were in need. Consider taking a moment to send an email or text thanking them.
4. Who are the people in your life whom God has called you to care for?

55

Naomi

Ruth 1:3–1:21 (from previous lesson)

In the previous lesson, we looked at the loving relationship between Ruth and Naomi. We saw how God blessed Ruth's loyalty to her mother-in-law. In this scripture, we witness Naomi's faith help bring Ruth, a Moabite woman, to know and worship the one true God and become a part of the lineage of Christ. We also see the hardship that widowhood brought to these women. Naomi is bitter and blames the Lord for her suffering. I believe that in her despair, Naomi showed authenticity in her faith. She did not gloss over her pain in her difficult circumstances. But even in her bitterness, she still recognized Him as her Lord.

When I'm in a hard season, I often feel like I should act a certain way because I am a Christian. I feel pressure to be an example of what it looks like to trust God. Yes, as believers, we are called to trust and be joyful in all circumstances; but let's be honest, this is easier said than done. We are humans. God knows this. People around us know it too. Trying to act like everything is wonderful when we are suffering inside is just that—an act. Sharing our feelings with trusted believers allows others to support us and pray for us. Showing this kind of vulnerability brings us into more authentic fellowship, which can, in turn, make others more open to sharing their struggles. By trying to play the *perfect Christian* role, we may inadvertently put up a wall between ourselves and others, both believers and seekers, making them afraid to come to us for fear of judgment.

Let's take off our masks and quit trying to act how we think we are *supposed to* act. Let's open up and let others walk alongside us in our hard times as we show grace and support to them in theirs. Life is better when we are in authentic relationships with other believers.

1. Do you feel pressure to hide your feelings of suffering? Why?
2. Do you have fellow believers that you can trust when you are going through difficult times? Do you feel comfortable asking for support and prayers?
3. Is there anyone in your life right now that may need grace-filled authentic fellowship? What can you do to reach out to them?

____

____

____

____

Women in Jesus's Inner Circle

What would it have been like to have a front-row seat during Jesus's ministry here on earth? Mary and Martha, along with their brother Lazarus, were friends of Jesus. They had the honor of visiting with Him and hosting Him in their home. And of course, Mary, the mother of Jesus, is one of the most revered women in the Bible. We will consider her perspective as the mama of our Lord and Savior, Jesus Christ.

Mary, Mother of Jesus

Luke 1:26–48

When I think of women in the Bible to emulate, Mary quickly comes to mind. If I had been in Mary's position when Gabriel told her she would give birth to Jesus, my reaction probably would have been one of disbelief and panic rather than obedience and praise. I have always struggled with caring too much about others' opinions of me. After the "How is this possible?" question, my next thoughts would likely have been, "How do I explain this to Joseph? Will my parents disown me? What is everyone going to think of me? The village gossips will surely have a field day with this." Mary responds, "I am the Lord's servant, and I am willing to accept whatever He wants. May everything you have said come true" (v. 38), demonstrating her trust, obedience, and submission to God's will for her life.

She also recognizes the extreme honor in this chosen role.

> Oh, how I praise the Lord. How I rejoice in God my Savior! For he took notice of His lowly servant girl, and now

63

generation after generation will call me blessed.

(Luke 1:46–48 NLT)

We see the strength of Mary's faith. From the moment she heard the news, she believed that she was carrying God's promised Messiah. She recognized Jesus was not only her son but also her Savior.

Mary's story reminds us that the qualities God values in people are so different from the values of this world. When God decided who would bring His child into the world, He did not choose a royal, highly educated, or wealthy woman. He chose a young peasant who was humble, obedient, trusting, and strong in her faith.

It took a special woman to birth and raise the Son of God. Think about the enormous responsibility she felt in rearing Him, an imperfect mother, caring for the only perfect being to walk the earth. It must have been bittersweet for Mary as she witnessed Jesus in His ministry, with intense motherly pride as he taught and performed miracles, along with anger and frustration as she saw many reject Him. Imagine her heartbreak as she watched Him die on the cross. Although Mary was likely overwhelmed and did not fully understand what this chosen role would involve when Gabriel gave her the news, she willingly made herself available to God's plan for her life.

1. Imagine yourself in Mary's situation. What would your reaction have been?
2. What do obedience and submission to God mean to you?

3. Is there an area in your life you feel that you are resisting obedience to God?

4. Has there been a time in your life when you obediently followed God's will even though you were scared?

____

____

____

____

____

____

____

____

____

____

Martha

Luke 10:38–42

I've heard this story many times and can relate to both characters. My desire is to be like Mary, not only with Jesus but also with other relationships in my life; however, the pressure to get everything done or have everything perfectly prepared often turns me into a Martha. Whether it's with Jesus or our loved ones, tasks, even those done in service to others, do not take the place of building relationships. Sometimes we can get so caught up in the details we end up neglecting the very people we are trying to serve.

I love to entertain because I enjoy spending time with my wonderful family and friends. I used to feel a lot of stress over the meal I would cook when having guests for dinner. Plus, cooking is not my favorite thing. Unfortunately, this often meant spending more time in the kitchen than with my guests. I've learned that keeping it simple and finding recipes where most of the work is done beforehand allows me to spend more time with the people I am hosting.

Another danger when we get caught up in making everything perfect is that we can become disappointed, even bitter when our efforts seem to go unnoticed. Martha is a prime example of this when she asks Jesus to come to her defense. She must have been surprised at his response. He points out that what He wants most is our hearts. Sometimes even our ministry can take us away from our relationship with Jesus. Just like Martha, we can feel tired, overworked, and start to feel resentful. At this point, our serving becomes more about us than about Jesus. We need to make sure our relationship with Him always comes first.

1. Do you tend to be like Martha? How so?
2. What tasks or details tend to pull you away from personal relationships in your life?
3. Are there areas of your ministry where your efforts to serve Jesus are causing you to neglect him?
4. If you have identified any relationships, spiritual or personal, where you feel your priorities have shifted out of balance, what can you do to help get things in proper order?

Mary, Sister of Lazarus and Martha

Luke 10:38–42 (from previous lesson)
John 12:1–8

Mary is an example of humility, submission, and complete adoration of Jesus. I can picture her sitting at his feet, gazing up at Him while he taught. When she poured the expensive perfume on Jesus's feet, Judas chastised her act of worship. Although the Bible points out that Judas most likely had selfish motives, one can see his practical point. Jesus advocated for helping the poor, but also He knew Mary's heart and recognized her gift.

In both scriptures, we see Mary being fully present with Jesus, appreciating and savoring every moment she had with Him. We have so many distractions today. (Yes, I'm looking at you, smartphone.) The world moves at a lightning-fast pace. We are often pulled in many directions at once. Being fully present in my relationships with God and the people in my life is a daily challenge. Though I am nowhere near mastering this, I will share what has helped me improve. It took me years to get into the consistent habit of setting aside quiet time each day to read the Bible and pray, but doing so has had a tremendous impact on my faith and relationship with God.

Each morning, before the rest of my family wakes, I pour a cup of coffee and curl up on the couch with my Bible or Bible app (as you can see, I have a love-hate relationship with my phone—so distracting, yet so convenient). It has now become a cherished part of my daily routine. During church services, my mind often races with my mental to-do list and other distracting thoughts. When I enter the sanctuary, I ask God to quiet my mind so I can worship Him with Mary-like adoration and learn what He would have me glean from the message.

Just as Mary recognized the importance of her time in the physical presence of Jesus, we should also be mindful that the time we have with our loved ones during our earthly life is limited. For those of us who are mothers, we only have a precious number of years that our children live under our roof when we have the opportunity to train them up in the way they should go. One way I have tried to be more fully present with my family is to make a concerted effort to put away my cell phone and ask my family members to do the same, at the dinner table, on car rides, and when we are spending time together as a family. Just before bed is also a great time to spend a few one-on-one moments with my children, ending with a nighttime prayer.

Being fully present with my husband can be hard simply because we are both busy and exhausted. When our children were young, having regular date nights was important for our marriage. Our wonderful babysitter, Miss Lisa, who became like family, was a blessing. Knowing our kids were in good hands and having a blast gave us a chance to go out, relax, and focus on each other. And when I get that precious time with my girlfriends or other family members, I make sure that spending time together takes priority over lavish preparations. Going for a walk can be a great way to spend time with God or someone you love while getting a little fresh air and exercise (bonus!). In whatever way you can spend time with God and the people in your life, work on being present in the moment.

1. What can you do to be more fully present in your relationship with Jesus?
2. Make a list of the important people in your life and write down ways to be more fully present in your time with them.

You can read more about Mary and Martha and their faith in John 11:17–44.

____

____

____

____

____

____

Stories of Redemption

The following lessons show us how God uses people regardless of their past mistakes and sins. Not one of us is beyond redemption. He loves us. He is for us. He paid the price so that we could be forgiven and be made new through the death and resurrection of Jesus Christ.

Rahab

Joshua 2:1–14
Joshua 6:22–25
Hebrews 11:31
James 2:25

In the Bible, this woman is referred to as Rahab the prostitute or, in some translations, Rahab the harlot. At no point in history have either of these titles been looked on with esteem. However, in Hebrews 11:31, Rahab is commended for her great faith. The Book of Matthew begins with a record of the ancestors of Jesus. Rahab is one of the few women mentioned by name in the genealogy. (Matthew 1:5).

Rahab is a wonderful example of how God can use people regardless of their status to glorify His kingdom. One might question why the Israelite spies chose to stay at her house. The location of her home, built into the city wall, made it a great place to gather the intel they needed. Due to Rahab's reputation, the men would be assumed to be customers and likely not raise suspicion by staying there. Knowing Rahab's faith, God led the spies to this safe haven. Rahab had heard about the miracles God performed for the Israelites. She believed their Lord was the supreme God and that He had given them this land. Rahab correctly assumed the Israelites would successfully conquer her city. Risking her own life to cover for the spies, Rahab shows she feared and served the same God they did. She recognized her opportunity to protect herself, as well as her family, from destruction.

Rahab's story shows that our sin does not have to define us. There is no sin so great that it is above God's redemption. Once we have confessed our sins, the Lord wants us to move forward, covered by His grace. He wants us to accept the gift of salvation and the freedom that comes with it. If you feel shame due to your mistakes and think that God can't use *someone like you*, think again. We are all sinners. God is looking for willing hearts, not perfect people, to build His kingdom. Sometimes our life experience, even the most painful and shameful parts, puts us in a unique position to minister to others.

This story also reminds us that we should not dismiss anyone as not open to hearing the good news. I admit there have been times when I've made assumptions based on a person's appearance or outward persona. Do you think these Israelite spies would have ever suspected this prostitute from Jericho would be in the lineage of their Messiah? There are people all around us who are in desperate need of God in their life. We should be open to relationships with people different from us.

Rahab was rewarded for her courage and faith. The Israelites kept their promise. Rahab and her family had protection when their city was destroyed. Rahab was able to rise above her reputation and save her family. She obeyed God, left her sinful career, and became a wife and mother, fulfilling her role in the lineage of Jesus.

1. Is there sin in your life or your past that is inhibiting your relationship with God? If so, pray that God will help you move forward under His grace.
2. How can you use your unique experience to serve God and minister to others?
3. Are there people you have previously dismissed with whom you may be able to plant seeds of the gospel?

Gomer

Hosea 1:2–3
Hosea 3:1–5

The marriage of Hosea and Gomer parallels God's relationship with the nation of Israel. God speaks to the prophet Hosea, telling him this and commanding him to marry a prostitute, warning him that she will be adulterous in their marriage. Imagine the prewedding jitters Hosea must have felt before marrying Gomer, knowing the hurt and shame their relationship would bring. Yet he obediently married Gomer and showed her mercy and grace when she betrayed him, just as God did to the people of Israel.

This scripture compares idolatry to adultery. When we worship idols other than the one true God, it is as if we are cheating on Him. Although idolatry may look different today (I doubt many of us are bowing down to gold statues or building sacrifice altars), it still exists. Idolatry occurs when the pursuit of earthly desires such as wealth, success, or vanity becomes foremost in our lives and robs our devotion to our Lord and Savior, Jesus Christ. Just as there is a line with adultery, there is a line with idolatry. Sometimes we don't recognize when we are approaching it or have crossed it. We are called to be good stewards of the resources God has given us. It is prudent to save wisely, but this can cross over into hoarding and making money our idol. The Bible tells us to work excellently at our job as if we are working for the Lord; but if we are so focused on climbing the corporate ladder that we put our careers before our relationship with God, our family, and our friends, success has become an idol.

People can become our idols. I'm writing this message on the heels of an extremely contentious election season in our nation. During this season, I watched people in both political parties put so much hope in their preferred candidates as if they had the power to change everything wrong in our world. Elevating mere humans to a higher than appropriate status, whether they are political leaders, religious leaders, or family members, can pull our focus away from God while setting ourselves up for a huge disappointment.

The beautiful overarching theme of Hosea and Gomer's story is redemption. Even after Gomer continually wronged Hosea, he still pursued her, forgave her, and brought her back to him. Their marriage is a picture of God's love and devotion to us. No matter how far we have strayed, He loves us, pursues us, and offers us redemption in a way that is hard for us to wrap our human minds around. I would have a hard time forgiving, let alone going after, my husband after multiple incidents of infidelity the way Hosea did with Gomer, but this is how God loves us and wants to redeem us.

And I am convinced that nothing can
ever separate us from God's love. Neither
death nor life, neither angels nor demons,

neither our fears for today nor our worries about tomorrow—not even the powers of hell can separate us from God's love.

(Romans 8:38 NLT)

1. Are there areas of your life that you worry can become idolatry?
2. When you read this scripture, is it hard to imagine the love, forgiveness, and redemption Hosea offers to Gomer?
3. Do you have a hard time believing God wants to extend this kind of love and grace to you?

Bonus reading: I recommend reading the book of Hosea to learn the story of God's love and redemption of the people of Israel. *Redeeming Love* by Francine Rivers is a beautiful retelling of Hosea and Gomer's story, symbolizing God's unconditional love for us.

____

____

____

____

____

____

Zelophehad's Daughters
(Mahlah, Noah, Hoglah, Milcah, and Tirzah)

Numbers 27:1–11

The story of Zelophehad's daughters demonstrates God's love for those whom society does not esteem. When Moses went to the Lord, He supported these women in a time when they did not have rights. God's proclamation, "If a man dies and has no sons, then give his inheritance to his daughters," was revolutionary. Previously, only sons had the right to inherit their fathers' land and possessions. Not only was God taking care of Zelophehad's daughters, but He also declared that this would be the law moving forward.

We see here the importance of advocacy. Although I tend to be conflict-avoidant, over the years, I have learned to advocate for myself and my family when necessary. (Mama bear has come out on more than one occasion.) I don't believe God wants any of his children to be marginalized or treated unfairly. Sometimes we are in situations where we need to stand up for ourselves. It may be an abusive spouse or an unfair teacher or boss. There is a difference between being humble and being a doormat.

To determine when we need to take action, we should first pray and seek counsel. If you feel action should be taken, go about it respectfully as these women did. Not only is it the right thing to do, but also we will likely have better results if we are calm and rational, backing up our case with concrete examples. Follow an appropriate order of escalation, first going to the person directly, then escalating it if that does not yield change. Recognize times when we may need to bring in someone to help advocate for us. Notice how Moses, their leader, brought their case to the Lord. Be willing to advocate for others when appropriate. We may be in a position to help support a parent, friend, or colleague. If our children are in a situation where they are being treated unfairly, we have an opportunity to guide them through what respectful advocacy looks like.

While on the subject of advocacy, I would be absolutely remiss not to talk about Jesus Christ, our ultimate advocate.

> But because Jesus lives forever, his priesthood lasts forever. Therefore, he is able once and forever, to save those who come to God through him. He lives forever to intercede with God on their behalf.
> (Hebrews 7:24–25 NLT)

> My dear children, I am writing this to you so that you will not sin. But if anyone does sin, we have an advocate who pleads our case before the Father. He is Jesus Christ, the one who is truly righteous. He

himself is the sacrifice that atones for our sins—and not only our sins but the sins of all the world.

(1 John 2:1–2 NLT)

Let's be honest, "if anyone does sin" is really "when anyone does sin." We all exhibit the human tendency toward sin. We all need Jesus, our Savior, our redeemer, our advocate. He came down from heaven; lived here on earth, fully God and fully human; suffered a criminal's death on the cross to purchase our freedom and salvation; and continues to intercede with God on our behalf for eternity. What a gift! What a Savior!

1. Do you remember a time when you had to advocate for yourself? How did you go about it? What were the results?
2. Think about the people in your life. Is there anyone who needs your help as an advocate?
3. Take a moment to reflect on Jesus as your advocate. Thank Him for His willingness to intercede on your behalf. If you have not accepted Jesus as your Savior, I encourage you to consider this amazing gift of salvation. Jesus is longing for you to accept this gift and take that first step of entering into a personal relationship with Him.

About the Author

Sherry is a wife and mother of two teenagers. She has a heart for encouraging others and helping them grow in their walk with Jesus, especially her fellow sisters in Christ. In addition to writing her blog, www.sherryblisshaase.com, she enjoys speaking at women's conferences. Sherry resides with her family in beautiful Northern California.